E.R. Violet Publishing, LLC
West Des Moines, IA 50266
violetpublish@gmail.com

Printed in the United States of America

Illustrations by Bill Love

Book Design by WORD**ART**, LLC West Des Moines, IA

PastorPickle.com

This book belongs to

_____

(A child of God)

Lessons for Living Series

Pastor Pickle
and the
Bumble
Bees

Bill & Lona Love

    The sound of the horn signaling the end of the high school basketball game between the Happy Hollow Hedgehogs and the Jericho Jellyfish filled the gymnasium. As the crowd stood and cheered, a familiar voice rang out from the public address system.

"The final score... Happy Hollow 74, Jericho 62. Thank you for joining us tonight. God bless you and please drive safely on your way home!"

Pastor Percy Pickle turned off his microphone, picked up his scorecard and sat back in his chair. Pastor Pickle loved basketball, having played it himself when he attended Happy Hollow High School many years ago. And now, when he wasn't tending to his duties as pastor of the **God Is Love Church** in Happy Hollow, Pastor Pickle volunteered as the public address announcer at all the Happy Hollow Hedgehog home basketball games.

As Pastor Pickle stood to leave, he heard, "Hi, Pastor Pickle," and turned to see Brendon and Bailey Bumble and their mother, Barbara Bumble.

"Well, hello," Pastor Pickle said to them with a warm smile. "That was sure an exciting game, wasn't it?"

"Yes, it was!" replied Barbara Bumble. "It's always good when the Hedgehogs win."

Pastor Pickle noticed Brendon and Bailey Bumble were each carrying a large paper bag and asked, "Have you been shopping?"

"No," said Brendon Bumble. "Our mom brought us to the game, but we're going to our dad's for the weekend."

"Oh?" said a surprised Pastor Pickle, looking directly at Barbara Bumble.

"Yes," said Barbara Bumble. "Their father and I aren't living together right now."

"These are things we're taking to our dad's apartment," said Bailey Bumble. "Our school work, our pajamas... stuff like that."

Just then, their father, Bradley Bumble, approached from the other direction.

"You're late!" snapped Barbara Bumble, scowling at him. "You were supposed to be here ten minutes ago!"

"I got here as soon as I could! I *do* work for a living, you know!" snarled Bradley Bumble.

Pastor Pickle stepped forward and said in a calm voice, "I'm sorry to hear about your situation. I know this is not easy for you or the kids, but here's something I want you to think about. I've counseled other children in similar situations and helped them sort through their feelings and concerns. I could meet with Brendon and Bailey Bumble at the church on Wednesdays after school if you think it would be helpful."

"I think it would," said Barbara Bumble.

"Yes," agreed Bradley Bumble. "I do, too."

The following Wednesday after school, Mrs. Stella Stencil, the church secretary, showed Brendon and Bailey Bumble into Pastor Pickle's office and they set their large shopping bags next to the door. Doogie, Pastor Pickle's dog, ran up to them and excitedly welcomed them, jumping up and down.

"Hello and welcome," smiled Pastor Pickle. "Please come in and have a seat." As they all sat down, Doogie stretched out next to Pastor Pickle's chair and almost immediately closed his eyes.

"I think we should begin with a short prayer," Pastor Pickle said and they bowed their heads.

"Precious Lord, thank you for these wonderful kids. We know you love each of them very much and want nothing but the best for them. Please help them feel safe as they sort through this confusing time. Give them strength and comfort and understanding and let them be very aware that they are never alone because of your unfailing love. We thank you for always being with us. Amen."

When Pastor Pickle opened his eyes, he saw that Bailey Bumble was wiping a tear from her cheek. "Bailey Bumble, tell me what you're feeling right now," Pastor Pickle said to her.

"I just don't understand why all this is happening," Bailey Bumble said quietly, wiping away another tear. "Why can't my mom and dad just get along? Was it something I did? Haven't I been good enough?"

"First of all," said Pastor Pickle, looking at both Brendon and Bailey Bumble, "you need to realize it's okay to feel sad about what's going on with your parents. Believe it or not, they are sad, too. It will take everyone a while to work through the sadness. But eventually, it will begin to feel better. I promise you that."

Pastor Pickle saw them look at each other.

"And the next thing you need to be very clear about," continued Pastor Pickle, "is that what you and your parents are going through is not in any way your fault. It has nothing to do with your behavior. Your parents will tell you this, too, if you ask them. What's happening between them is grownup stuff... grownup stuff that you probably won't understand until you're adults yourselves. But it's very important that you believe none of this is your fault. Period. Do you believe this?"

They both looked at Pastor Pickle and nodded.

"Good!" Pastor Pickle said. "And I want both of you to know that you will always be loved. First, and most importantly, loved very deeply by God, who will never stop loving you and has promised to never leave your side. He will always be there for you."

"But do you know who else loves you very much?"

"My mom?" replied Bailey Bumble.

"Right!" said Pastor Pickle. "And also your dad! They both love you very much and just because they may be having problems with their relationship with each other, it will never change the way they feel about you. Not one bit! They will always be your mom and dad, even if they are no longer married to each other. And they will always love you, just like God will always love you."

Pastor Pickle stood and walked over to a large white tablet on an easel. "As we meet over the next few weeks," Pastor Pickle said, "I'm going to give you a list of helpful things to consider and here's the first one."

He wrote on the white tablet in big letters, **BE CONFIDENT!**

"I want you to be confident about several things. First, as I just said, you can be confident that you are loved. Second, you can be confident that none of this is your fault. And third, you can be confident that everything that seems so uncertain right now will eventually be okay. You can be confident of all these things because that's God's plan for you. So, any time you start to feel sad or scared or angry or hurt, remind yourselves to be confident."

BE CONFIDENT!
✓ You are loved!
✓ It is not your fault!
✓ Everything will be OK!
✓ God is always with you!

They talked for a while longer about being confident and then Pastor Pickle said a prayer and they collected their bags and moved toward the door. Doogie began running in circles around Brendon and Bailey Bumble as they went outside to wait for their dad to arrive.

The next week, when Brendon and Bailey Bumble arrived at the church, they saw Doogie chasing a bee around in the yard and got to laughing so hard at him they almost dropped the large shopping bags they were carrying. As they walked into Pastor Pickle's office and put their bags down, Doogie dashed by them, claiming his place next to Pastor Pickle's chair and began scratching his ears.

After saying a short prayer, Pastor Pickle asked, "You seem happy today. How did it go this week at home?"

"Better," replied Bailey Bumble. "Our mom told us you were right. No matter what, she and Dad are always going to love us."

"But I have a question," said Brendon Bumble with a concerned look on his face. "I know they both love me, but sometimes my dad makes me feel like I shouldn't love my mom. But I do."

"Yeah," agreed Bailey Bumble. "It hurts when they say mean things about the other one in front of us. I really don't want to hear it. It feels like they want me to choose sides."

"It's unfortunate when they express their frustrations with each other in front of you," said Pastor Pickle. "But it's a very confusing time for them, too. They don't mean to make you feel sad, but sometimes they don't realize how what they say makes you feel. But you don't have to choose sides. It's okay to love them both."

Pastor Pickle got up and moved to the big white tablet where he had written **BE CONFIDENT!** last week. Beneath that, he wrote in big letters **BE HONEST!**

Turning back to Brendon and Bailey Bumble, Pastor Pickle said, "One of the best ways you can show your love for your parents is to be honest with them. Talk to them about your feelings when you're sad or mad or confused or feeling uncertain. Be honest with them about not wanting to hear bad things about your other parent. Remember, they both love you. So love them back by being honest with them."

"I haven't been very honest with my friends either," admitted Bailey Bumble. "I've been telling my friend Zoey Zingerman that my dad was out of town a lot on business, because I'm embarrassed about our parents not living together. I finally got honest with her and told her the truth during recess one day."

"And what was her response?" asked Pastor Pickle.

"You'll never guess what Zoey Zingerman said! She thanked me for being honest and told me not to be embarrassed, because she had gone through the same thing a couple of years ago when her parents got a divorce. She said she knew exactly how I was feeling. Zoey Zingerman is a really good friend!"

"Oh, that's wonderful," said Pastor Pickle. "See what happens when you trust others enough to be honest with them? They're your friends because they care about you and want to be there for you."

Pastor Pickle looked toward the door and smiled as an older boy walked in.

Doogie saw him, too, and ran to greet him.

"Brendon and Bailey Bumble, this is Stretch Stackhouse," said Pastor Pickle, motioning for the boy to join them. "Because you both go to the Happy Hollow basketball games, you already know he's the star player on the Hedgehog basketball team. I asked him to join us today because he has some things he would like to share with you."

"Well, I'm here today because Pastor Pickle asked me to tell you my story," began Stretch Stackhouse. "About eight years ago, I was in the same situation you're in today. My parents decided to get a divorce and my father moved out. I have to admit I was pretty scared and confused at first. I was about your age at the time and I remember wondering if my parents were still going to love me. If they were living apart, where was I going to live? Where were my things going to be? And what about my dog, Tank?"

Doogie perked up when he heard Tank's name and looked around. But when he didn't see Tank, he closed his eyes again.

"I had lots of questions and not many answers," continued Stretch Stackhouse. "Fortunately, Pastor Pickle helped me talk with my parents and, over time, most all of my questions got answered."

"Where did you end up living?" asked Brendon Bumble.

"Well, I found out I didn't need to worry about that," answered Stretch Stackhouse, "because instead of having only one home, I suddenly had two. My mom kept our house, so I still had my bedroom there, and my dad moved to an apartment, where I had a new bedroom... *and* a swimming pool!"

"What about your toys?" asked Bailey Bumble.

"I took some of them to my dad's place and kept some of them at Mom's. In time, I had things at both places. Because my dad couldn't have pets at his new apartment, we agreed that Tank would live at my mom's house. So fortunately I didn't have to split Tank in half," Stretch Stackhouse said with a wink as he glanced at Doogie.

They all laughed and Doogie covered his eyes with his front paws as if he understood what they were laughing about.

"The thing I learned during that time in my life was that there were going to be a lot of changes," continued Stretch Stackhouse. "But Pastor Pickle helped me realize the answer to dealing with all the changes was not for me to be worried, but for me to be flexible."

At that, Pastor Pickle stepped to the big white tablet and under **BE CONFIDENT!** and **BE HONEST!** he wrote **BE FLEXIBLE!**

"Being flexible means adjusting to your new arrangements and conditions as they change and learning to embrace them rather than resist them," said Pastor Pickle.

"For instance," said Stretch Stackhouse, "now I had two homes, but the rules were different at each place. I had to help wash the dishes at my dad's because he didn't have a dishwasher. I was expected to take the garbage out at one place but not the other. My bed times were also different at each place. Learning to be flexible made it much easier for me to adapt to all these changes. In fact, eventually I began to look at every change as a new adventure!"

Brendon and Bailey Bumble looked at each other and smiled.

"Another helpful thing Pastor Pickle taught me was the difference between the things I *wanted* and the things I really *needed*," said Stretch Stackhouse.

"What do you mean?" asked Brendon Bumble.

"For instance, you might *want* something, but ask yourself if it's really something you *need*. I wanted an electric toothbrush at Dad's, like I had at Mom's. But I eventually realized that all I really needed was a toothbrush. You may want the latest trendy jacket, but all you really need is a jacket. Do you see the difference?"

Pastor Pickle said, "*Wants* are simply wishes. But *needs* are real. It's important that you recognize the difference. It's all part of being flexible in your new circumstances."

Stretch continued, "After a while I got used to the new arrangements and everything pretty much became routine again. I knew what to expect and the confusion and anxiety finally went away. I could tell that my parents both were happier and I realized that they never stopped loving me and wanting the best for me. Just like God does!

"One last thing," said Stretch Stackhouse, "and this is really important! Know that God will always be there for you. Pastor Pickle taught me that and it's a good thing for you to always remember."

Pastor Pickle thanked Stretch Stackhouse and then said a prayer. As they all walked toward the door, Stretch Stackhouse gave Brendon and Bailey Bumble high-fives.

Doogie darted outside, eager to continue his pursuit of that pesky bee. As they watched Doogie running in circles and chasing the bee, Pastor Pickle had an idea.

The following week, as Brendon and Bailey Bumble walked up the sidewalk toward the church, they saw Doogie growling at the bee as it landed on the front step. After giving the bee a final bark, Doogie followed everyone into Pastor Pickle's office.

Brendon and Bailey Bumble put their big paper bags down and moved toward their seats. Doogie took his usual spot, sprawling beside Pastor Pickle's chair and closed his eyes.

"Looks like Doogie has found his favorite spot," laughed Bailey Bumble.

"Yes, he has a lot of favorite places," said Pastor Pickle. "Here in my office he loves to be next to my chair. At the playground, he's usually lying in the shade under the merry-go-round."

"He's funny!" laughed Brendon Bumble.

"He sure is," agreed Pastor Pickle. "But do you know why Doogie always goes to these favorite places? It's because he feels safe there. Feeling safe is important to all of us, including Doogie. Have you noticed that we all sit in the same chairs week after week when you come here?"

Brendon and Bailey Bumble looked at each other and realized he was right.

"You probably do that because experience has taught you that you feel safe knowing that everything around you is familiar. There's something unsettling about the unknown, isn't there?"

"Yes," agreed Brendon Bailey. "That's why we were a little bit scared when our mom and dad split up. Once we knew how it was going to work, we felt safer again."

"Right," said Pastor Pickle as he went to the big white tablet and under **BE CONFIDENT!** and **BE HONEST!** and **BE FLEXIBLE!**, he wrote **BE SAFE!**

Turning back to Brendon and Bailey Bumble, Pastor Pickle continued, "Feeling safe is very important to feeling happy. So, when what you're used to gets disrupted and you're not sure what to expect next, it's natural to feel sad and even a little scared.

"Do you know why you feel safe here at church?" Pastor Pickle asked. "It's because you know God is here. But he's not just with you here at church. He's with you everywhere and always. So one way to begin feeling safe again when you're feeling afraid is to talk to God. Pray to him and ask him to help you. He loves it when you ask for his help and he'll make you feel safe again."

"I always feel better after I pray," said Bailey Bumble.

"Can you think of anyone else who makes you feel safe?" asked Pastor Pickle.

"My grandpa, Bernard Babbitt," said Brendon Bumble. "He is a great guy and I love hanging around with him!"

"My best friend, Zoey Zingerman," added Bailey Bumble.

"That's wonderful! It's important that you have someone, in addition to a parent, you can feel safe talking to about your feelings when you're not sure about things. It can be a friend, a relative, a teacher... even a pastor!" Pastor Pickle said with a wink and a grin.

Just then, Pearl Pickle, Pastor Pickle's wife, walked into the room carrying a large cardboard box. Doogie immediately woke up and ran to her, jumping and wagging his tail!

"Hi, kids!" Pearl Pickle said to Brendon and Bailey Bumble, as she set the box on Pastor Pickle's desk. "Pastor Pickle and I have a little surprise for you."

As Brendon and Bailey Bumble walked up to the desk, Pastor Pickle and Pearl Pickle each reached into the box and pulled out a bright yellow backpack and gave them to Brendon and Bailey Bumble.

"For weeks now I've seen you lugging those large paper shopping bags around, and last week when we were watching Doogie chasing that bee outside, I had an idea. I thought if you had these bright yellow backpacks on, you would look just like bees."

"Bumblebees!" shouted Brendon and Bailey Bumble. "We love them!"

"You can use these backpacks to carry your things back and forth between your parents' houses," said Pearl Pickle.

"We've been talking about things that you should be," Pastor Pickle said, pointing toward the big white tablet. **"BE CONFIDENT! BE HONEST! BE FLEXIBLE! BE SAFE!** Maybe we should call these the '**BUMBLE BEEs**.'

Then Pearl Pickle added another "**E**" to each item on the list, making it read, **BEE CONFIDENT! BEE HONEST! BEE FLEXIBLE! BEE SAFE!**

They all laughed and just then, the bee that Doogie had been chasing flew in through the open window and landed on Doogie's nose. Doogie growled and crossed his eyes and they all laughed even harder!

A Message From **Pastor** **Pickle**

Throughout life, we're faced with situations we wish we could avoid. Divorce is certainly one of those situations. Divorce is not God's plan for anyone, but he assures us he will walk with us through any journey we may take. So he will always be there for us.

Remember the BUMBLE BEES when you approach any difficult situation in your life and especially if your parents are having issues in their relationship. Regardless of their feelings for each other, know that their love for you hasn't changed. So your love for them shouldn't change either. Love is a choice, not a feeling. We can choose to love people, even when they do things that disappoint us, just as God loves us regardless of the mistakes we make.

When you find yourself dealing with uncertainty and confusing emotions, remember the one you can always count on -- your Heavenly Father. Talk to him about your worries. He loves to hear from you!

Say this prayer with me:

Dear God

Thank you for always being with us. Help us to understand our up-and-down feelings. Guide us in our choices and let us show love to others, even if we don't always feel like it. Help us to be more like you. We confidently pray all these things with very grateful hearts.

Amen

Additional References

"For I know the plans I have for you," says the Lord. "They are plans for good and not for disaster, to give you a future and a hope."
Jeremiah 29:11 (NLT)

Always be humble and gentle. Be patient with each other, making allowance for each other's faults because of your love.
Ephesians 4:2 (NLT)

No power in the sky above or in the earth below-- indeed, nothing in all creation will ever be able to separate us from the love of God that is revealed in Christ Jesus our Lord.
Romans 8:39 (NLT)

He is my loving ally and my fortress, my tower of safety, my rescuer. He is my shield and I take refuge in him.
Psalm 144:2 (NLT)

Additional References *(cont.)*

Search for the Lord and for his strength; continually seek him.
1 Chronicles 16:11 (NLT)

He renews my strength. He guides me along right paths, bringing honor to his name.
Psalm 23:3 (NLT)

For God has said, "I will never fail you. I will never abandon you.
Hebrews 13:5 (NLT)

Made in the USA
Columbia, SC
18 March 2018